Imagine a Bird

Stanford Apseloff

OHIO DISTINCTIVE PUBLISHING

Columbus, Ohio

For Evan and Ryan

ISBN: 978-936772-27-8

One can learn much from our feathered friends,
By looking through a long camera lens,

See how each of them looks and acts,
Take good notes, learn some facts.

But most of all, please have a good time,
Imagining birds as you read each rhyme.

(Red-headed barbet)

King penguins

Imagine that penguins inhabit a city.
With so many birds, it's not very pretty.

The streets are more crowded than New York's Times Square.
Everyone's standing—no room for a chair.

Kea

Imagine a parrot that likes to play,
Tossing small stones that are put in its way.

As he plays this game, all the while,
The glint in his eye is akin to a smile.

Hummingbird

Imagine a bird that's as light as a penny,
With legs so short you'd doubt it had any.

Lilac-breasted roller

Beware the rainbow, a dazzling show,
Wet as fresh paint—go above or below.

Imagine a robin or common thrush
Ever so careless, in such a rush,
Soars through a rainbow instead of around.
See how he looks when he reaches the ground.

Weka

Penguins, we know, are unable to fly,
But imagine some others that dare not try.

The weka and takahe live on the ground.
New Zealand's South Island is where they are found.

Takahe

Pretend that the birds are like people you know.
Some are quite chatty, some nod hello.

Some are as quiet as a proverbial mouse.
Some are alone. Some have a spouse.

Let's take a look and see what we see.
It's time for some fun—I think you'll agree!

Yellow-crowned night heron

One does his absolute best to impress,
Fluffing his feathers without much success.

Hyacinth macaws

Hyacinth macaws gossip and chatter,
About local news and things that matter.

Black skimmer

Here's one who likes to stand out in a crowd,
Wearing an outfit that's much too loud.

Scarlet macaw

Here a most unlucky fellow
Left his home with no umbrella.

King penguins

Imagine what penguins do day after day.
Is all of it work, or is some of it play?

How would you like an adventure or two
In water so cold it would make you turn blue?

Adelie penguin

Would you like surf crashing over your head?
Or bellyflop diving from icebergs instead?

Adelie penguins

Or maybe, just maybe, a long barefoot hike
Up boulders of ice is what you would like.

These penguins are fit to do this and more,
Coming and going from sea to the shore.

Gentoo penguins

Imagine a bird that flies through water
With skill that surpasses even the otter.

Cormorant

When a cormorant strikes a perfect pose,
You have to wonder whether she knows

A camera lens is aimed her way,
To catch the fleeting display.

Macaroni penguin

A macaroni penguin sleeps in the snow.
What is she dreaming? I do not know.

Penguins have feathers—she's one step ahead,
'Cause she has no need for a featherbed.

The snow would feel frigid for you and me,
But she sleeps, maybe dreams, quite blissfully.

Adelie penguins

Think bottle feeding's quite a chore?
Watching this makes my throat feel sore.

Adelie penguins do their best
To feed the youngsters in their nest.

Yellow-billed oxpeckers

Think horseback riding is lots of fun?
Try a zebra instead in the noonday sun.

Oxpeckers often catch a ride
And peck small insects from the animal's hide.

Resplendent quetzal

So which of our friends is the fairest of fowl?
It could be the quetzal; it isn't the owl.

The resplendent quetzal is a beauty so rare,
That if you should see one, you surely would stare.

Burrowing owls

Imagine two owls that sleep underground,
Not is a tree, but beneath a small mound.

Toto toucans

Picture a bird, a most beautiful creature—
Imagine its beak is its best facial feature.

The toto toucan totally rocks,
With elongated bill orange-red like a fox.

Potoo

Imagine a tree branch that opens its eyes.
It's a potoo revealing a clever disguise.

Great egret

Imagine some birds that can fish with their beak.
What kind of fish do you think they would seek?

This great egret's skill is second to none
As he fishes for lunch in the noonday sun.

Yellow-crowned night heron

This heron is happy with just a small taste.
Do you think there's a chance he is watching his waist?

African fish eagle

Imagine an eagle swooping toward prey.
Critters below all scamper away.

Various backyard birds, Costa Rica

Colorful birds perched in a tree,
It's rare to behold such diversity.

Red-throated bee-eater

On the banks of Zambezi lined thickly with trees,
A bee-eater bird feeds on insects like these.

Rufous-tailed jacamar

Picture a giant of a hummingbird
With the prettiest voice you've ever heard.

They call him a rufous-tailed jacamar.
He fans his feathers—he knows he's a star.

His body is nearly ten inches long,
And the jacamar sings a trill-like song.

Chinstrap penguins

Picture chinstrap penguins making lots of noise,
Talking all at once, like very naughty boys.

Gentoo penguin

A male gentoo penguin helps build a fine nest
With finishing touches designed to impress.

Adelie penguin

Imagine lands of ice and snow, shaped by wind and spray.
At the shore a penguin roams—done fishing for the day.

Magnificent frigatebird

Imagine you're flying in perfect splendor,
Gliding with wings that are long and slender.

Scarlet macaw

Imagine a bird that's fire-engine red
From the tip of its tail to the top of its head.

A bird that is stately and even more regal,
Than fabled phoenix or the grandest of eagle.

The scarlet macaw is a New World treasure,
It's value in gold?—no one can measure!

Caracara

Picture a raptor with wings stretched wide,
As sunlight shines on its underside.

The caracara feathers are striped white and brown.
This bird hunts for prey from the sky and the ground.

Pelicans

Picture a paddling pelican pair.
They're waiting for fish—have you any to spare?

Roseate spoonbills and white ibis

Imagine a sunset with magical light
On waters reflecting a wondrous sight.

Spoonbills lend pink to water so still,
As ibis flies by with its telltale bill.

Osprey

Imagine soaring beneath the clouds,
High above any gathering crowds.

Atlantic puffin

Puffins are plump, with rather short wings.
Are puffins huffin' when flapping those things?

They dive to great depths for eels, hake, and herring
To feed the young puffins for whom they are caring.

Collared aracari

Picture a bird beneath a red flower
With a piece of banana it's about to devour.

Buff-necked ibis

Spiders, frogs, and snails, a high-protein diet—
It's tasty to the ibis, but don't you ever try it.

Agami heron

The agami herons are rather shy.
Hide in the shadows—I don't know why.

They hunt for fish under cover of brush,
They wait, and they watch, and they never rush.

Jabirus

Imagine a bird standing five feet high,
With a nine-foot wingspan to help it fly.

This largest of stork is the jabiru.
Parenting duties?—the father helps too.

Chinstrap penguins

Word from the lookout—the coast is clear.
The party goes on—there's nothing to fear.

Mockingbird with marine iguana

Imagine a dragon's your very best friend.
No one would bully you ever again.

King penguins

Picture a perfect penguin parade.
Imagine the awesome colors displayed.

There's safety in numbers—and if anyone cares,
Their number exceeds two-point-two-million pairs.

South Georgia pintail

Is one of the ducks disrespecting the other?
I wonder if he is the younger brother.

Blue-footed boobie

Imagine a bird with blue legs and feet.
Can you guess what this bird most likes to eat?

Sardines and mackerel, anchovies too,
And other small fish off the coast of Peru.

Northern gannets

Point-four-trillion birds live on our planet.
Including the elegant northern gannet.

At the top of a cliff, in the wide open air,
Romance is blooming for one lucky pair.

Roseate spoonbill

Imagine a bird with a spoon on its face.
A fork or a knife would look out of place.

And this much I'll say, in case you've not heard—
The more that it eats, the pinker the bird.

Tui

Imagine a bird with a white-feathered chin,
A fan-shaped tail, and a beak black and thin.

It lives in New Zealand, a land down under.
I tell you this now just in case you should wonder.

Tern

One tern needs to learn she won't find fish in the snow.
If she wants food for herself or her brood, to the ocean she must go.

Yellow-billed hornbill

Picture a bird with a banana-like beak,
From Botswana, Zimbabwe, and Mozambique.

The yellow-billed hornbill is quite a sight.
When it flaps its wings and the nose takes flight.

Look for birds near, or far away.
Hear their songs on a summer's day.

They're out there, waiting—you will see.
Flying above or perched in a tree.

And if you don't find what you're looking for,
The ones that you think you most adore,

Then this you can do instead anywhere—

Cedar waxwing (photo taken in my backyard in Ohio)

Imagine a bird. Imagine you're there.